T0365872

A Collection

THE STORY OF AMERICA IN STAMPS
IN
STORYBOOK FORM

THE MAKING OF AMERICA

The Premiere Collection

By Frank McCullers

DEDICATED TO
KAMARO*BRYAN*DIANA
EUGENIA
KATELYN*JASMINE*ALEXIS
THE LOVES OF MY LIFE

WHILE THESE ARE NOT THE OPINIONS
OF A SCHOLAR
SOME THINGS ARE PLAIN TO SEE

IT'S SIMPLE–IT'S EDUCATIONAL
IT'S OUR HISTORY

SPECIAL THANKS TO MY
DAUGHTER
KAMARO
FOR ALL HER HELP

To order additional copies of this book, contact:
Xlibris
844-714-8691
www.Xlibris.com
Orders@Xlibris.com

ISBN: Softcover   978-1-4134-3898-7

Print information available on the last page

Rev. date: 01/28/2022

A
Collection

@FMCKCB

THE PREMIERE COLLECTION

THE MAKING OF AMERICA
TAKES YOU ON A VOYAGE
A MOST REWARDING READING
THRU THE PAST - PRESENT - FUTURE
THE STORIES STAMPS TELL
FROM BUTTERFLIES TO ELEPHANTS
FROM VIETNAM TO DESERT STORM
THE STAMPS TELL THE STORY
FROM GEORGE WASHINGTON TO SADDAM
FROM 3 OLYMPICS TO CHRISTMAS (62)

SHARE THIS WITH YOUR CHILDREN

By F. McCullers

NAME

(   )

STORYBOOK COLLECTION

A SEED OF LOVE WAS PLANTED
AND FROM THAT LOVE GREW A CHILD
NOW I -NOT BEING OF GREAT WEALTH
DID WONDER--WHAT I COULD GIVE....
Ahhhhh--A COLLECTION
AN INVESTMENT ($) IN THE MIND
A STORY THEY WILL NEVER FORGET
A TRIP THAT'S REALLY A VOYAGE
THROUGH THE PAST PRESENT AND FUTURE
FROM THE WONDERFUL WORLD OF STAMPS
TURN THE PAGE AND COME ON INTO
A MOST REWARDING READING
READ THE STAMPS AND ENJOY THE JOURNEY

AMERICA

HOW IT ALL BEGAN

FROM THE EXPLORER
TO SPACE

(COLUMBUS)
TO
(APOLLO)

THE PATH MAN CHOSE

PIONEERS

DISCOVERY

"SETTLEMENT"

"STATEHOOD"

"REVOLUTION"

ALL THE STATES OF AMERICA
THE UNITED STATES

ONCE UPON A TIME
THERE WAS A LAND OF
OPPORTUNITY
AND ALL THE BIRDS SANG

FROM
NORTH CAROLINA
TO
CALIFORNIA

North Carolina
USA 20c
Cardinal &
Flowering Dogwood

Missouri
USA 20c
Eastern Bluebird & Red Hawthorn

West Virginia
USA 20c
Cardinal &
Rhododendron Maximum

New York
USA 20c
Eastern Bluebird & Rose

Nebraska
USA 20c
Western Meadowlark & Goldenrod

Oregon
USA 20c
Western Meadowlark & Oregon Grape

Massachusetts
USA 20c
Black-Capped Chickadee & Mayflower

Arkansas
USA 20c
Mockingbird & Apple Blossom

Michigan
USA 20c
Robin & Apple Blossom

Wyoming
USA 20c
Western Meadowlark & Indian Paintbrush

Mississippi
USA 20c
Mockingbird & Magnolia

Wisconsin
USA 20c
Robin & Wood Violet

Pennsylvania
USA 20c
Ruffed Grouse & Mountain Laurel

New Mexico
USA 20c
Roadrunner & Yucca Flower

South Dakota
USA 20c
Ring-Necked Pheasant & Pasqueflower

Connecticut
USA 20c
Robin & Mountain Laurel

Rhode Island
USA 20c
Rhode Island Red & Violet

Delaware
USA 20c
Blue Hen Chicken & Peach Blossom

Virginia
USA 20c
Cardinal & Flowering Dogwood

New Hampshire
USA 20c
Purple Finch &

13

THE EXPLORER'S

MODES OF
TRANSPORTATION

FROM
STAGE-COACH
TO
FAST CARS

THE SOUNDS OF
PROGRESS

FLAGS OF AMERICA

THEY ALL CAME TOGETHER
UNDER THE SAME FLAG
AND SOME OF THEM WERE
FREE

ONE NATION
YOUR OWN BELIEF
AND FREE

JUSTICE FOR ALL

14

FREE THE HOSTAGES

WE HOLD THESE TRUTHS

(RIGHT TO VOTE)

(RELIGIOUS FREEDOM)

(LIBERTY FOR ALL)

(EQUAL RIGHTS)

JOBS
THE CREATION OF OPPORTUNITY

YOU CAN BE ANYTHING YOU WANT TO BE

EDUCATION
&
DETERMINATION

"SET YOUR GOALS"
&
"REACH YOUR PEAK"

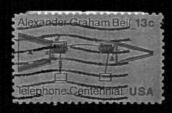

THE PRESIDENTS
AND
THE ONES THAT COULD HAVE BEEN

THE FAMOUS
AND
NOT SO FAMOUS

THE PEOPLE WHO HELP MAKE IT ALL POSSIBLE

THEY ALL MADE THEIR CONTRIBUTIONS TO SOCIETY AND AMERICAN HISTORY

23

SCIENTIST

POETS

PHYSICIANS

CHEMIST

TEACHERS

POLICEMAN

Harriet Tubman
Black Heritage USA 13c

Carl Sandburg
USA 13c

1757 La Fayette 1957
3¢
United States Postage

Bobby Jones
USA
18c

Robert Millikan
37c
USA

UNITED STATES POSTAGE
ANDREW CARNEGIE
4¢

UNITED STATES POSTAGE
3 CENTS 3

UNITED STATES POSTAGE
HORACE GREELEY
4¢

UNITED STATES POSTAGE
2

WILLA CATHER

WILLA CATHER

UNITED STATES POSTAGE
2 CENTS 2

UNITED STATES POSTAGE
3 CENTS
WILLIAM ALLEN WHITE

CHAMPION OF LIBERTY
RAMON MAGSAYSAY 1957
PRESIDENT OF THE PHILIPPINES
8¢
UNITED STATES POSTAGE

USA
15c
Gen. Bernardo de Gálvez
Battle of Mobile 1780

ELIZABETH BLACKWELL · FIRST WOMAN PHYSICIAN
US POSTAGE 18c

20c
USA
TREATY OF AMITY AND COMMERCE BETWEEN USA AND SWEDEN 1783

George Mason
USA 18c

Lafayette
US Bicentennial 13c

AMERICA'S ARCHITECTURE
&
FAMOUS LANDMARKS

ABC TO XYZ

Mies van der Rohe 1886-1969 Illinois Inst Tech Chicago
Architecture USA 20c

Walter Gropius 1883-1969 Gropius House Lincoln MA
Architecture USA 20c

Frank Lloyd Wright 1867-1959 Fallingwater Mill Run PA
Architecture USA 20c

Jefferson 1743-1826 Virginia Rotunda
Architecture USA 15c

Eero Saarinen 1910-1961 Dulles Airport Washington DC
Architecture USA 20c

Strickland 1788-1854 Philadelphia Exchange
Architecture USA 15c

Library of Congress USA 20c

Latrobe 1764-1820 Baltimore Cathedral
Architecture USA 15c

Touro Synagogue Newport RI 1763 USA 20c

"To bigotry no sanction, no persecution, no assistance."
—George Washington

Stanford White 1853-1906 NYU Library New York
Architecture USA 18c

Bernard Maybeck 1862-1957 Palace of Arts San Francisco
Architecture USA 18c

Richard Morris Hunt 1828-1895 Biltmore Asheville NC
Architecture USA 18c

SAN XAVIER DEL BAC MISSION U.S. 8c
HISTORIC PRESERVATION

Richardson 1838-1886 Trinity Church Boston
Architecture USA 15c

DECATUR HOUSE U.S. 8c
HISTORIC PRESERVATION

EDUCATION

IS THE

KEY

THE FABRIC OF SOCIETY
BUILDING OF THE MIND

KNOWLEDGE

IS

POWER

America's
A B C
Libraries
X Y Z
USA 20c
Legacies To Mankind

Glow by Josef Albers USA 15c
Learning
never ends

Letters
Preserve
Memories
USA 15c

Write Soon
USA 15c

Wise shoppers
stretch dollars
**Consumer
Education**
USA 20c

IT ALL DEPENDS ON
ZIP CODE

P.S.
Write
Soon
USA 15c

Letters
Lift Spirits
USA 15c

HIGHER EDUCATION
UNITED STATES POSTAGE 4c

EDGAR LEE
MASTERS
AMERICAN POET
UNITED STATES 6c

Letters
mingle souls
Donne Raphael
10c US

বাংলাদেশ ২
A B C D
BANGLADESH

Edna St. Vincent Millay
American Poet USA 18c

Universal
Postal Union
1874-1974 Chardin 10c US

Universal
Postal Union
1874-1974 Hokusai 10c US

10c
US
THE LEGEND OF SLEEP

US
POSTAGE
Sixth International
Philatelic Exhibition
Washington D.C. 20008

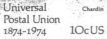

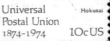

THE ARTS
&
THE ARTIST

Pennsylvania Toleware
Folk Art USA 15c

18 28 39

GILBERT & SULLIVAN
The Yeomen of the Guard

GILBERT & SULLIVAN
The Mikado

GILBERT & SULLIVAN
Iolanthe

Acoma: School of American Research
Pueblo Art USA 13c

Pennsylvania Toleware
Folk Art USA 15c

29

NAT KING COLE

Heiltsuk, Bella Bella
Indian Art USA 15c

13c Folk Art USA Quilts

Folk 13c

USA Dance Modern 13c

USA Dance Theater 13c

San Ildefonso: Denver Art Museum
Pueblo Art USA 13c

JIMMIE RODGERS
Performing Arts USA 13c

THE BARRYMORES
Performing Arts USA 20c

GEORGE M. COHAN
Performing Arts USA 15c

13c Folk Art USA Quilts

COLONIAL AMERICAN CRAFTSMEN
UNITED STATES POSTAGE 8 CENTS

METROPOLITAN OPERA
1883 1983 USA 20c

USA 20c
James Hoban White House Architect

SPORTS

BUILDING OF THE BODY AND MIND

"BASKETBALL" "BASEBALL"

"HOCKEY" "BOXING"

"ARCHERY" "VOLLEYBALL"

"SKATING" "SWIMMING"

"TRACK & FIELD"

33

THE
GAMES
MEN
&
WOMEN
PLAY

THE
JET AGE

(ENERGY BUSTER)

CELEBRATE
PHILADELPHIA
BIRTHDAYS

Orville and
Wilbur Wright
Aviation
Pioneers

USAirmail 31c

USA 13c

50th Anniversary Solo Transatlantic Flight

Commercial Aviation

USA 13c   1926·1976

Wiley Post
Aviation
Pioneer

USAirmail 25c

THE
SPACE AGE

FROM THE MOON TO MARS

NO BOUNDERIES LEFT UNEXPLORED

9^{95} USA

25th Anniversary   First Moon Landing, 1969

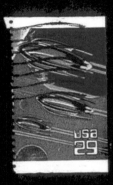

USA
29

EARTH LANDSAT   29 USA

USA
29

First Moon Landing, 1969

SATURN VOYAGER 2   USA
LECT STAMPS

PLUTO NOT YET EXPLORED   29 USA

INTERNATIONAL SPACE YEAR 1992 $1.05
E... EAM
MAI... CENTRE
VI... 3130   AUSTRALIA

INTERNATIONAL SPACE YEAR 1992 $1.20
AUSTRALIA

ARCH TRIANGLE
... DURF
CHAPEL HIL
USA
29

URANUS VOYAGER 2   29 USA

SPACE

MARS   *VENUS*

JUPITER

SATELLITE
SPACE STATIONS
SPACE SHIPS

CONSERVATION
&
PRESERVATION

LETS HOPE ITS NOT TO LATE

WILDLIFE

ANIMALS
&
PLANTS

(ELEPHANTS)
(LIONS)   (TIGERS)
(EAGLES)

(FOREST & FLOWERS)

44

AMERICAN BALD EAGLE

AFRICAN ELEPHANT HERD

USA 18c

CHIPMUNK

USA 13c

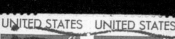

UNITED STATES 6c

UNITED STATES 6c

AMERICA'S WOOL

AMERICA'S WOOL

WILDLIFE CONSERVATION

PRONGHORN ANTELOPE

UNITED STATES POSTAGE 3c

UNITED STATES

TROUT 8c

WILDLIFE CONSERVATION

WILDLIFE CONSERVATION

WHOOPING CRANES

US POSTAGE 3c

MOOSE

USA 13c

FLUSHING

Organized Labor
Proud and Free

USA 15c

Save Wetland Habitats

USA 18c

USA 18c

Selva Lacandona
UNIDOS PARA LA CONSERVACION

1000 PESOS   Jaguar

M E X I C O   1991

Selva Lacandona
UNIDOS PARA LA CONSERVACION

1000 PESOS   Jaguar

M E X I C O   1991

RED FOX

USA 13c

RACCOON

USA 13c

THAILAND

10 POSTAGE

Canada 17

45

BIRDS & BEES

MOUNTAINS
&
TREES

CONSERVE & PRESERVE

HONOR OUR SOLDIERS

OUR CHILDREN DIE FOR OUR FREEDOM

RESPECT
OUR
VETERANS

FREEDOM IS YOUR REWARD

29 USA
Buffalo Soldiers

© USPS 1993

CONTINENTAL MARINES   AMERICAN MILITIA

US   10c   US   10c

CONTINENTAL NAVY

US   10c

USA 20c
Medal of Honor

USA · 15c

HONORING VIETNAM VETERANS
NOV · 11 · 1979

THE NATIONAL GUARD OF THE U.S.
IN WAR   IN PEACE

THE OLDEST MILITARY ORGANIZATION IN THE U.S.

29
USA

Allies land in North Africa November 1942

29
USA

Congratulates
To The
Cause

U.S.
8c

Sybil Ludington   Youthful Heroine

Veterans
Administration

VA

Fifty
Years of Service

USA 15c

1863 INTERNATIONAL RED CROSS 1963

5c   UNITED STATES POSTAGE

MAN & WAR

POLICY
&
OIL

AFGHANISTAN

IRAQ

VIETNAM

KOREA

UNITED NATIONS

HOPE FOR PEACE

IF NOT IN MY LIFE TIME
MAYBE YOURS MY SON

FOREIGN COUNTRIES

WE ARE THEY
IT IS FROM WHERE WE COME
IT IS OUR HISTORY

IT'S WHAT AMERICA IS MADE OF

AMERICA IS A BLEND
A MIX WITH NO END

41 CHANNEL TUNNEL

41 CHANNEL TUNNEL

DRESSES OF PAKISTAN
PUNJAB
Rs.6

Cadena de las Americas
MEXICO $2,000
AURELIO PEREZ   AMATE   1992

35c SINGAPORE

35
12TH COMMONWEALTH SUMMIT CONFERENCE
ΚΥΠΡΟΣ CYPRUS KIBRIS

50 Rs.
ISLAMIC REP. OF IRAN   50 Rs.

BRASIL
TARIFA POSTAL NACIONAL
1° PORTE   SERIE A

ANNEE DE L'ENFANT
REPUBLIQUE D'HAITI   1.25

Commonwealth of the
Northern Mariana Islands
LATTE STONES
USA 29

INDIA
75TH ANNIVERSARY OF THE JALLIANWALA BAGH MARTYROOM
1994

CHILDREN'S ART
JAMAICA
CHRISTMAS 1991
$1.10

REPUBLICA DE HONDURAS
Correo Aéreo   L.0.15
1902-1977
Homenaje a la
Organización
Panamericana
de la Salud
75 Aniversario
Abastecimiento Agua, Area Rural

TANZANIA----PERU

NIGERIA------POLAND

HRVATSKA--PAKISTAN

(LANDS YOU NEVER KNEW EXIST)

WE MUST HELP THOSE LESS FORTUNATE THAN WE ARE

BUT FOR MY BELIEF GO I

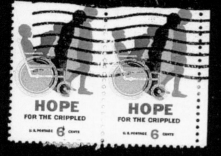

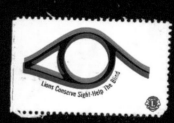

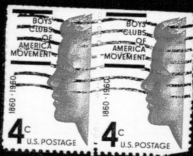

LOVE

**SHARE THIS WITH A
CHILD
FRIEND
BROTHER
SISTER
MOM & DAD**

***KEEP THE FAITH*
*IT'S OUR HISTORY***

Printed in the United States
by Baker & Taylor Publisher Services